You Can Make It,
I Know You Can

Common
Love -

You Can Make It, I Know You Can

Lynette Comma

VANTAGE PRESS
New York

Cover design by Susan Thomas

FIRST EDITION

Copyright © 2004 by Lynette Comma

Published by Vantage Press, Inc.
419 Park Ave. South, New York, NY 10016

Manufactured in the United States of America
ISBN: 0-533-14753-0

Library of Congress Catalog Card No.: 2003096890

0 9 8 7 6 5 4 3 2 1

To my two sons, Trevor Jr. and Steven Comma

Contents

Acknowledgments   ix

A True Friend   1
Lord, Help Me to Wait   2
Waiting on the Lord   3
We Must Walk on the Streets of Pain and Suffering   4
You Can Make It, I Know You Can   6
Our Life Is in God's Hands   8
Let's Stay in the Heart of Valentine   9
Love Is an Expression of Love   10
God Made a Deposit of Love   11
Rapture of Love   12
A Mother's Love   14
A Tribute to Fathers   16
Dance of Victory   18
Lord, I Give You Thanks   19
Christmas Is Here Again   20
The Trick of Halloween   23
Satan Will Do the Time   24
There Is Hope beyond the Grave   25
Death Could Not Keep Me in the Grave   26
Seek Me First   28
Little Boys Are Adventurous   29
Young Ladies Are Beautiful like Daisies   30
A Woman of Honor   31
Respect Is Needed Wherever You Go   32

Mom, Please Don't Let Me Go to School   33
The Voice of Innocence   34
Perseverance   35
I Thank You, Doctor King   37
Mr. Ben   39
Summer Is Here Again   40
Haymarket Day   42
The Raging Storm   44
War on America   46
My Shiny Basketball Home Court   49

Acknowledgments

I thank my God for giving me the inspiration and strength to write these poems.

I thank my two sons, Trevor Jr. and Steven, for their constant compliments.

Special thanks to Pastor Alton J. Beech and his wife, Tina Beech, along with the Greater Anointing Harvest Church for their continuous support.

I also want to thank Minister Marvena Graham for editing, S.P.A.C.E. organization, and Lynette Barnes for being there for me.

You Can Make It,
I Know You Can

A True Friend

God sends friends into our lives
for many reasons
especially when we are going
through a test in our season.
Life's journey was not meant for
one to travel alone.
This design was orchestrated from
the Master's throne.

Who can really find a true friend?
Someone on whom one can depend.
When adversity drifts along your way,
your comrade will not sigh and walk away.
Like a pillar of strength,
your friend will take a stand
and wait to see what is in
God's hand.

A true friend will respect the
attributes of your personality.
It does not matter what's one's
nationality.
When you place a desperate call
during the night,
your friend will join you in the
midst of your plight.
When you have done something wrong,
Your friend will forgive you
and tell you to be strong.

Lord, Help Me to Wait

Lord, my heart is surrounded by an
ocean of pain.
Looking through my eyes at the
circumstances,
I do not see much gain.
My feet are planted on a platform
of quicksand.
I am sinking pretty fast.
Precious Lord, please take my hand.

What I hold so dear to me is
slowly slipping away.
God, please help me to understand.
I just don't know what to say.
In my mind are many questions.
Holy Spirit, be my guide.
Lead me in the right direction.

Lord, I fall upon my knees,
Asking you for an abundance of grace.
Place in me a desire to constantly
seek your face.
At the end of every test, there
is a blessing.
When will this crisis be over?
Why am I guessing?

Waiting on the Lord

Star: Lord, I am in this trial for
          so long.
          My soul feels like it's gone.
          I am in a state of desperation.
          Please, Father, why the hesitation?

Father: My child, sometimes I work in seasons,
          read my word, it has so many reasons.
          I have seen your tears.
          Yes, I know all your fears.
          But you must go through the test.
          Remember I told the devil you
          are the best.

Star: Father, I have a confession.
          I feel such a great depression.
          Forgive me for my disbelief.
          I know if I meditate on your word,
          I will have a flow of relief

Father: My servant, I will not give
          you more than you can bear.
          You can look at the storm
          and not be consumed by fear.
          My presence will be with you
          wherever you go.
          For now and eternity, it will
          always be so.

We Must Walk on the Streets of Pain and Suffering

Pain and suffering are no stranger to
this Christian life.
They will dwell among us until the day
we die.
Who can escape their invasion?
Sometimes we take every precaution
to shelter our hearts form a head-
on collision.

On this road of affliction once
travelled the Lord of all.
He is capable of placing a
cushion beneath
to protect us whenever we fall.
He wrestled with the feeling of agony,
during his visit to the Garden of
Gethsemani.
This He subdued with a spirit of surrender.
His love for humanity remains so tender.

Lord, help us to understand that there
is a purpose to one's destiny.
Like Joseph of old, who was subject
to much scrutiny,
it was an experience that gave birth
through pain.
Look at the outcome that followed.
Life is not all in vain.

I will learn to wait for my
deliverance
in a world that shows little tolerance.
Instant gratification is the name of
the game,
trusting in the Lord from day to day.
How could life remain the same?

You Can Make It, I Know You Can

You can make it,
I know you can.
Evil's head may arise.
Satan is trying to orchestrate
your demise.
Folks are spreading vicious lies.
God will never never leave your side.

You can make it.
I know you can.
Your life may appear as if it were
aiming for zero.
Place no confidence in your feelings.
In God's history book, you are a hero.
God will never never leave your side.

You can make it.
I know you can.
Your tears go up to heaven at night.
You try to do the Lord's work right.
Another day will soon be gone.
God will say, my servant, well done.
He will never leave your side.

You can make it.
I know you can.
Jabez had a friend named sorrow.
There is hope for today and tomorrow.
Stay in the race.
Embrace God's amazing grace.
God will never never leave your side.

You can make it.
I know you can.
This trial that you are going through
makes you feel that it is only you.
All over the world there is
suffering and pain.
Your waiting is worth the
everlasting gain.

You can make it.
I know you can.
Don't you let go.
Let God's healing virtue flow.
Weeping may endure for a night,
But joy comes with the morning light.

Our Life Is in God's Hands

We were once children,
playing in the sand.
We did not know
our life was in God's hands.
Each time we went to bed
at night,
His presence was there like
a guiding light.

There were so many accidents
that could have escorted us to
the grave.
You chose to keep us in the
land of the brave.
Around us was always a hedge
of divine protection,
one that kept us going towards
the right direction.

We were chosen before the
foundation of this world.
Our lives are so much more precious
than gold, rubies, and pearls.
Every life has a divine purpose.
Lord, help us not to lose
sight of our main focus.

Let's Stay in the Heart of Valentine

You are my valentine.
Like the lovely red roses
that appear on a vine,
I welcome you into my web.
We can spend some time
spinning some thread.
Later on we can nibble
on a piece of bread.
Please have a glass of wine.
"Baby," let's stay in the heart
of valentine.

You are my valentine.
Please try to read between the lines.
I want our love to last forever.
Such thinking is so very clever.
No one should try to come between us.
We are stuck in a glue that is so glorious.
Let us stay in the heart of
true valentine.

Love Is an Expression of Love

Love made a decision to die
on a cross
on behalf of a world that is
dying and lost.
Love's eyes are always open
to see the needs of God's chosen,
to minister to those who
feel forsaken.

Love throws its arms around
the lonely widow.
Love prays for her continually
whenever trouble follows.
Love is moved with compassion
when someone weeps.
Those who will inherit the earth
are the humble and the meek.
Love never tries to seek out the
worst in others.
Encourage the best gift in your
sisters and brothers.

God Made a Deposit of Love

Who can really explain eros,
phileo, and agape love?
The creator himself,
God up above.
He willingly and unselfishly
offered his Son as a sacrifice
in order for mankind to live
forever in heaven's paradise.

Love is the arm that embraces
the prostitute,
that feeds the destitute.
It encourages the fortitude
then compliments the gratitude
while coping with the vicissitude.

God made a deposit of love in the
core of every heart.
Satan works hard to tear it apart.
Love will conquer the demons
of hate.
Jehovah will bring deliverance.
It is never too late.

Rapture of Love

There is chaos everywhere.
Evil is making its mark
all over the atmosphere.
Accepting Christ as Savior?
Men and women think twice.
The consequence of one's choice
is indeed an awful price.

The church is engaged to a man
named Christ,
preparing herself to marry
the groom.
Come aboard while there is
still room.
The wedding feast is about to
take place.
For every waiting moment,
God adds more grace.

Saints get weary.
Some have lost hope.
People ask God to help
them to cope.
Encouraging each other is a
perfect way to grow.
Faith will come alive.
Courage and strength will
continue to flow.

Heaven is our eternal reward.
The sound of the trumpet
some glad morning we'll look
toward.
Pain and suffering will be a
dream behind.
Everlasting joy
my soul will find.

A Mother's Love

Who can explain a mother's love?
The one who made it possible.
The Saviour up above.
She brought me into this world
through pain.
Her labor was not all in vain.

Both day and night,
she kept my diapers dry
and kissed my head when I tried.
Often she wiped the tears from
my eyes.
As I grew older,
she tapped my hands if I
told any vicious lies.

The day arrived when Mum sent
me to school
to learn the golden rule
so I don't become a fool.
The bullies were there to
terrorize my life.
Mother came to the school.
She said she'd not allow evil to strive.

Finally I got involved in the
dating scene.
Mum said, Follow your heart
may God fulfill all of your dreams.
The person may be short,
the person may be tall.
It's your choice to make after all.

Mother is growing wiser every day
to her grandchildren.
She has so much to say.
When her work here on earth is
finally done,
her memories will still live on
even when she is up and gone.

A Tribute to Fathers

There wouldn't be children in this
world, if there weren't any fathers.
It was rooted in God's plan to
deposit on the earth
a living creature He called man.
Ordained by God after all
to lead the family
to which he was called.

Father, a mighty warrior,
born to be a conqueror,
one who lovingly led his
family, through the valleys
of life.
He tries to avoid the pitfall
of strife.
God has given him the spiritual tools
to follow all the gospel rules.

When Father is near,
there is no need to fear.
All demons and witches will have
to disappear.
I can sleep throughout the night
because I know that whomsoever
comes through that door,
my dad will send him sailing on
a flight high, high, high.

God is able to stabilize fatherhood
in the midst of every neighborhood.
May all fathers answer the call
to lead their families by precept
and example
in a world that is evil and unstable.
God will have his final say
on that great resurrection day.

Dance of Victory

The doctors scheduled a day for
my surgery.
To be honest I considered this
situation to be perjury.
Well, they thought I had cancer,
I have always considered myself
a dancer.
I got up on my feet
and declared the devil a major
defeat.
I did a dance of victory,
trusting in Jesus,
the man who died on Calvary.

It's been two weeks after
the operation.
My body was still in a state
of recuperation.
The look on the doctor's face
confirmed what I already knew.
There were no signs of cancer,
not even a few.

Lord, I Give You Thanks

Lord, I give you thanks
for being so good to me
throughout the year
when so many things have happened
to cause me to fear.
Each morning you quicken my
mortal soul to arise.
You help me to live life
without having to compromise.

Lord, I give you thanks
for giving me a shelter
over my head.
If it was not for your mercy,
I would have been homeless instead.
When I look at the food on my table,
I say a prayer for the hungry
and the disabled.
My clothes closet is filled to capacity.
Lord, I thank you for all your
generosity.

Lord, I give you thanks
for the gift of my family,
for your host of protection,
from the heavenly
friends you have placed within
our pathway.
Saints that encourage me from
day to day.

Christmas Is Here Again

Christmas is here
yet another year.
The world will celebrate the
birthday of a King.
Church choirs lift their voices
to sing.
For God sent his only Son from
heaven above
to die on a cross through
unconditional love.

There seems to be a tidal wave
of gladness
looking through the hearts of
people everywhere.
The spirit of giving, sharing,
romancing, is in the atmosphere.
Neon signs flash their Christmas
lights.
Blinking tree bulbs dance with the
reflection on every window,
creating an appearance
so very bright.

The moon and the stars seem to
give accent to the light blue sky.
Pedestrians gaze with curiosity
as couples search each other's eyes.
Could it be a marriage proposal?
A genuine confession
or maybe a speech seasoned with
intense compassion?
The birds on the tree chirp with
one accord.
They are giving thanks,
Saying, Jesus is Lord.

Cooks are making the best shopping deals,
planning how to prepare the holiday meals.
Turkey, ham, chicken, with baked potatoes,
carrots, lettuce, and green peppers
harmonize with red slices of tomatoes.
Rice hooked up with beans of every kind,
guava, sorrel, gingerbeer, and others
follow close behind.

The eyes of children everywhere
show an expression of laughter and joy.
Little boys and girls count down
the final days,
anxiously waiting for that
favorite toy.
Colored gift boxes lend beauty
to the Christmas tree.
The youths carefully manipulate
its contents,
hoping for a chance to see.

Christmas is here again.
God came down to save mankind.
In Him there is hope and peace
to find.
His love dwells among people
of all races,
causing a smile on the countenance
of many faces.
Rejoice, rejoice, let the earth
rejoice,
to make Christ your Saviour is
a matter of choice.

The Trick of Halloween

Halloween, Halloween,
lurking in the dark,
hiding, seeking to devour
in the park.

Halloween, Halloween,
the demons are out tonight,
looking to see if there
are children within sight.

Halloween, Halloween,
Hell-fire is waiting for you.
Your tricks and your treats
will not hold back your defeat.

Satan Will Do the Time

Well, Satan, I see that you are up
to our old tricks again,
seeking whom you may inflict with pain.
In your board meetings, you talk about
organized crime.
I know that God will cause you
to do the time.

Every day you give out your assignment.
Your plan is for mankind to disobey
God's commandments.
You send your weak demons to trick
the believers.
Your stronger angels are released to
attack the preachers.

In my possession are the weapons that
will send you away.
The blood of Jesus will not allow
you to stay.
The fervent prayer of a righteous man
availeth much.
If God maintain a hedge of protection,
who can you really touch?
I have the sword of the spirit in my hand.
The Word of God will always stand.

There Is Hope beyond the Grave

Mom and Dad,
I am sorry to see you go.
You told me that death is
a sweet sleep.
You said you did not want
my soul to weep.
I see no fear upon your faces.
My Savior must have given
you more grace.

I treasure all the moments
that we once shared,
laughter, holidays, tears, sacrifices.
It simply showed that you cared.
You were brave enough to say
good-bye.
The Bible says that it is impossible
for God to lie.

These words are to those who are
left behind:
Don't let your spirit be saturated
with sorrow.
There is always hope for your
tomorrow.
God has the power to raise the dead.
Why should you worry?
Why should you dread?

Death Could Not Keep Me in the Grave

You called me all kinds of names.
I never tried to make any claims
to fame.
You spit all over my face,
but my Father up above gave me
extra grace.
Upon my head you placed a crown
of thorns.
You treated me with so much scorn.
Then you pushed a spear into
my side.
My love for you I'll never hide.

You drove the nails into my hands
and feet,
but the power of darkness fell
flat with defeat.
A legion of angels would have
given heed to my call
and wiped you off the earth for
once and for all,
but I willingly sacrificed my
life on the cross for you.
Would a friend do the same?
Only a few.

You could not keep me in the ground.
Mary and Martha sought for me, but
I could not be found.
My people, I give you authority over
the prince of adversity.
My blood that was shed on Calvary
will be your only security.

Seek Me First

You said you'll do whatever
it takes
to get riches and fame.
Life will not be the same
when you lay hold to your claim.

You said you want some fancy cars,
limousines, and lots of land.
Live on the beach
and lie on the beautiful sand.

You said you want to travel all
over the world.
Collect precious stones.
Gather genuine pearls.

God said, Seek me first, and
my righteousness.
I will guide you into my holiness.
The treasures I will give to you
will be blessings to others too.

Little Boys Are Adventurous

Little boys are created with a strong
drive for aggressiveness.
    Climbing tall trees.
    Chasing busy bees.
    Wiping dripping noses
    on their sleeves.
    Raking green and
    yellow leaves.
    Pitching little blue
    marbles.
    Riding on horse saddles.

What a fascination with trains,
playing with each other inside
muddy drains.
Fancy trucks with big wheels,
enjoying each other's yells and
screams.
Basketball and football.
That includes swimming and
running.
Oops! Someone just had to fall.
Flying kites way up in the sky.
It's an art everyone wants to try.

How about chasing little girls?
Oh, no! Not enough time for
those many curls.
Fighting for each other's toys.
Later on it's all destroyed.
A trip to the zoo is a very
good place to start.
Parents are so very, very smart.

Young Ladies Are Beautiful like Daisies

What would the world be
without young ladies?
Their beauty stands out
Like a garden filled with daisies.
Rooted in their voices is the
cry of innocence.
Their trail of obedience will
lead to the doors of recompense.

What would the world be without
young maidens?
Looking for adventure,
a life of sweet haven.
Mother is right behind to give
her support.
Dad is waiting for the final
report.

What would the world be without
young women?
Once upon a time they were
children,
sheltered in a school of learning
and preparation
leads them to a place of marriage
celebration.

A Woman of Honor

I am a woman **of beauty,**
sent to the planet earth
called to fulfill a duty.
A crown of honor I will wear
upon my head.
Nagging, rebelliousness I
choose to reject instead.

I am a woman **of dignity.**
There is no room in my heart
for enmity.
The bread of idleness I will
refuse to eat.
Keeping the home clean
I think is pretty, pretty neat.

I am a woman **of destiny.**
Spiritual and emotional growth
will guide me into perfect harmony.
To touch someone's life in a
positive way
brings purpose and meaning from
day to day.

I am a woman **of integrity.**
Many of the roads I travel
are built on a highway of complexity.
However, I will maintain a state
of positivity.
My defense is the roadblock
guarding against inferiority.
I will ride on the wings of faith.
Starting over is never, never too late.

Respect Is Needed Wherever You Go

Respect has always carried
itself with such elegance,
ready and willing to be
available when given a chance.
Respect does not discriminate
against anyone
and is always missed
whenever it's gone.

Respect is always needed in
the schools.
Many parents tell their children that
respect is Mr. Cool.
There is little tolerance for those
who disobey the rules.
Respect will discipline the ones who
behave as stubborn as a mule.

Respect likes to hang out
at the workplace,
to see the expression on every face.
When the boss gives out the assignment,
who will follow all the alignment?

Respect will take you among
kings and queens,
creating opportunities for
you to be seen.
Whoever teaches about respect is wise.
The rewards and benefits should
not be a surprise.

Mom, Please Don't Let Me Go to School

Mom, please don't let me go
to school.
My friends will think that
I am a fool.
I feel something in my throat.
There is a spot of dirt on my coat.
Mom, don't let me go to school.

Mom, please don't send me to school.
I had a very bad dream.
Can I have some ice cream?
How about some cake
and a piece of bake?
Mom, don't let me go to school.

Mom, please don't let me go to school.
Let me go outside.
I want to play and hide
and never, never come inside.

The Voice of Innocence

I was only five,
still trying to thrive.
You taught me how to respect.
That is what I recollect.
You showed me how to obey authority
to all law-enforcement security.

Now what am I supposed to do
when I am confronted by you?
You came to me as an angel
of light.
"Good God Almighty,"
I did not know how to fight.

Now I am fully grown,
just as lovely as a bunch
of flowers.
No! It did not take a couple
of showers.
I was cleansed with the blood of
the Saviour.
My soul is blessed and highly
favoured.

Perseverance

I did not ask to come into this world.
Of course that is what I have been told.
However, now that I am here,
I have a strong need to learn.
Show me the channels, and the tools.
I will certainly carry them to school.
Teach me the fundamentals of life.
This knowledge will enable me to thrive.

I have no time for limitations.
Stay away from me,
You "doors of hesitation."
I have been assigned to the destiny
of my calling.
To allow myself to be distracted,
it would really be appalling.
I will stay focused towards the
ultimate goal
The reward that I will reap
is yet to unfold.

The grass is green.
At least that's what it seems.
This is my perception.
I am going in that direction.
A career path is one of my
selection.
I believe this is a wonderful
conviction.

The "pebble of learning" is always
growing.
Please don't stop your stream
from flowing.
Advanced technology has invaded
our society.
Take advantage.
Make it a priority.
Let the ride of ambition take
you to the sky
and one of these mornings your
wings of visions will fly.

I Thank You, Doctor King

I can ride the bus
without making a fuss.
There are people of many races,
some of them with interesting faces,
blending their splendid colors,
as they ride the morning train.
Who can really ask for much?
I thank you, Doctor King.

In my thoughts lives a giant.
There is no need for me to
be defiant,
for there is no limitation
to what I can become.
Could be a doctor, lawyer,
manager.
Here I come.
I thank you, Doctor King.

I can go to school.
There is no set rule.
I can achieve my ultimate dream.
We can all take a dive in this stream.
When the rewards are given out,
on that wonderful day,
you can walk across the stage
and proudly say
I thank you, Doctor King.

I long to see the valley
of change,
for there is still hidden
the shadow of hate.
I will push down its ugly head
and override it with love instead.
Hope must be kept alive
that one day we all will strive.
Thank you, Doctor Martin Luther King.

Mr. Ben

I have been in love with Ben
for quite a long while.
Ben is so versatile.
He is a depiction of style.
Ben is well known wherever
he goes.
Women reach out their hands
to grab him.
I try not to become sensitive.
Neither do I make any foes.

It is always a delight
to be in Ben's presence.
He possesses a sweet odor,
one that can become very intense.
People abuse him for many reasons.
There is a great demand for him
throughout all seasons.

Ben likes to travel all over
the world.
So many stories of him have been told.
Many times I run into Ben at a restaurant.
Sometimes I see him at the market.
I simply pick up Mr. Ben's Rice
and put him in my basket.

Summer Is Here Again

The birds flapped their wings
through the blue sky.
Soaring along the summer wind,
they did fly.
The green trees stand like
soldiers side by side.
Squirrels find a refuge, a
place they can run and hide.
Flowers of many colors dance
to the music of the warm air.
The sound of buzzing bees
seems so very near.
Summer is here again.

People seek release from the
scorching heat.
Inside the buses, not even
an empty seat.
Air-conditioned rooms are the
places to be.
Skirt chasers toot their horns,
searching for an opportunity
to see
a pretty girl on the street.
Summer is here again.

Ice cream plasters children's faces.
Parents caution their young ones,
to bend down and tie their laces.
The playground contains an
attraction of rides.
The atmosphere is filled with
laughter, as youths come down
the slides.
Summer is here again.

Youngsters jump in and out.
Fire hydrant shoots its water spout.
Swimming pools, beaches, embrace
their inhabitants.
Only the disobedient decide
to become defiant.
The great demand for bottled water,
leaves the store shelves empty.
Everyone including babies must
consume plenty.
Summer is here again.

Drivers blast their music
so very loud.
Men walk with their women,
shoulders held up proud.
Looking for a taxi cab
surely makes you frown.
Summer is here again.

Haymarket Day

Today is haymarket day.
The sun pushed the clouds
aside to say,
"I am big.
I am bright.
Please let me show off my light."
The wind came by and shook the
trees from side to side.
There was no place the birds could
run and hide.

The vendors are wearing their
sombrero hats.
Wooden boxes and stools.
That is where they sat.
Market structure is commercialized.
Their prices are advertised,
ready to make the best deal.
Anticipating that their produce
will make a good meal.
Colorful fruits and vegetables are
stacked up in different rows.
Convenience is the way to go.
Customers won't have to bend so low.

The sound of paper bags, tinkling coins
is everywhere.
There is a smell of fish, and pineapple
in the atmosphere.
One-hundred-dollar bills, fives, tens, ones.
Circulate from hand to hand.
Men and women stand in line.
The smiles on their faces seem to
indicate that they understand.

It's the end of another haymarket day.
The sun peeps through the blue sky
then decides to go away.
Boxes of fruits and vegetables are
scattered everywhere,
sold for a dollar here,
sold for a dollar there.
Vagrants came and filled their bags.
One night spent with food is better than rags.

The Raging Storm

I looked through my window on
that cool evening.
The sky appeared so very dark.
Children started leaving the park.
Trees were dancing from side
to side.
Squirrels went out to search
for holes to hide.

All of a sudden there was an
abundance of rain.
I said, "Lord, thank you, the
water will clean our drains."
The thunder rolled and rolled
like a huge giant walking
across the sky.
I grabbed my pillow.
I did not want to cry.

Like fireworks the bolt of
lightning flashed across the heavens.
I ran to the next room,
praising God for giving me a safe haven.
There was no need to switch on the lights.
Inside and outside looked so very bright.

I gazed at the pattering of the
raindrops on the roadside.
Stranded pedestrians raised their
hands, hoping the cabs would give
them a ride.
Cars with sirens raced through the traffic
to reach their destinations.
Motorists went about their modus
operandi, without hesitation.

The storm climaxed throughout the
night.
I thought to myself, *What an
awesome sight.*
This is a reminder that there
is a God up above,
ready and willing to show us
his love.

War on America

It was an ordinary day
September 11th,
the year 2001.
America conducted business
in a normal way.
Terrorist invaders possessed with evil
smashed huge airplanes into the "hearts"
of the Twin Towers.
Thousands met death face to face,
changing the course of history.
Oh, grave, where is your victory?

The Twin Towers
represent the symbol of financial
strength and patriotism,
descended into shattering fragments
towards the ground.
Perpetrators, whose hearts are enveloped
with hatred and fanaticism,
carried out their vicious plans.
People were running everywhere.
Smoke and fire darkened the atmosphere.

Dwelling in the midst of adversity
emerged the spirit of community
and generousity.
The Salvation Army, the Red Cross,
nurses, doctors, firemen, National Guard,
civilians, and many more
together worked in unison to find
and assist survivors.
The crowd cheered whenever someone
was rescued to life.
There was no room to entertain feelings
of strife.

The President is prepared to bring
the criminals to justice.
The country is willing to stamp
out the images of prejudice.
This message is for the world to see
America the brave
must stay the land of the free.
Nations stretch their arms out to
support.
"The war against all Americans"
will be fought.

Spirituality resurrected itself
into the hearts of people everywhere.
Men, women, and children congregated
themselves into churches.
They looked for answers.
They came to share.
Pastors all over the nation
preached messages of consolation.
Souls are smiling in heaven.
Awaiting the final revelation.

My Shiny Basketball Home Court

My home ball-court is like
a friend to me.
It gives me hope and dreams
to see.
Every day
I do not delay.
I come down to the "court"
and I say, "What a nice day."
I dribble some more, and some more,
not poor, but light, and then
I score.
I dribble some more, and more,
and more.

I concentrate
then I jump high in the sky.
I shoot, swish, and swish.
Sometimes my throat gets dry.
Today is the big game.
My first game.
The "court" shines.
I leave my mistakes behind.
I play with the big guys
and in my mind I say the line,
"I can do it."
"I can do it."

All through the game it was
the same.
Swish! Swish! Swish!
Like you never heard before.
All of a sudden, I am lifted
up in the sky
People are yelling.
They are whistling.
Boston wins.
Boston wins.